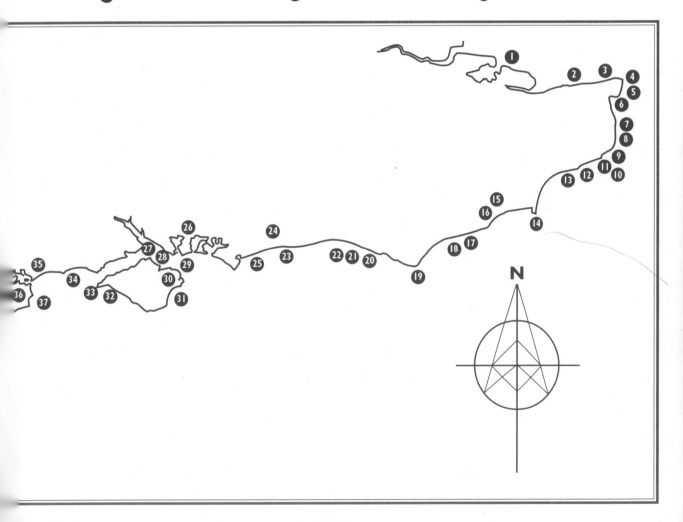

Tom Soper

Islington   1997.

A VOYAGE
ROUND GREAT BRITAIN

Sheerness to Land's End

To Shirley

A VOYAGE
ROUND GREAT BRITAIN

Sheerness to Land's End

by

David Addey

in the footsteps of William Daniell R.A.
(1769-1837)

Foreword by Lord Chorley
Chairman of the National Trust

SPELLMOUNT LIMITED
Staplehurst

British Library Cataloguing in Publication Data:
A catalogue record for this book is available
from the British Library

Copyright © David Addey 1995

ISBN 1-873376-34-0

First published in the UK in 1995 by
Spellmount Limited
The Old Rectory
Staplehurst
Kent TN12 0AZ

1 3 5 7 9 8 6 4 2

Typeset in 11/12 Baskerville by SX Composing Ltd,
Rayleigh, Essex

Printed in Hong Kong

GENERAL NOTE

Except for some minor adjustments, the extracts from William Daniell's extensive narrative are as written by him. His spelling of certain names and words that were in common usage at the beginning of the 19th century has been maintained.

His exploration of the coast from Sheerness to Land's End, which constituted the seventh and eighth stages of his Voyage, commenced on July 27th 1822 and finished on September 12th 1823. I arrived at Sheerness on the first stage of my Voyage on 31st August 1988 and reached Land's End on September 14th 1990.

ACKNOWLEDGEMENTS

My gratitude must be expressed in two parts. First, to Martyn Gregory for suggesting that I should undertake this Voyage; to friends, old and new who have given me encouragement, refreshment and accommodation – sometimes at embarrassingly short notice; and to all those who have manifested their interest in the project by purchasing many of the paintings. My thanks, also, to the owners of properties who have given me access to the Daniell viewpoints, without which it would have been impossible to complete the first two stages of the project.

Secondly, to those who have given me valuable assistance in the preparation of this volume. Tourist information offices, museums, local historians and total strangers have willingly provided information on many of the locations and subjects. The owners of several of the paintings have kindly returned them to me for photographing, while others, in this country and abroad, have had their's photographed for me; such willing co-operation has ensured that every scene depicted in these two stages has been included. My sincere thanks, also, to John Henderson, who, in his retirement, delights in literary pursuits and has given shape and cohesion to my text, and to Peter Humphreys of Wells Graphics for his expertise in the photography of many of the paintings.

FOREWORD

(by the Chairman of the National Trust)

We are an island people accustomed to the sea and often take for granted easy access to the coast. David Addey's watercolours remind us of the scenic beauty of our shores by paralleling with the work of William Daniell and prompt questions about its history and future.

Over the centuries, our country has been threatened by invasion and we have stood ready to defend the coast. Fortifications, lookouts and gun sites are familiar features that occur in David Addey's work. At the same time, the sea has always been a source of food, thus providing a livelihood for fishing communities. We have always been a trading nation, reliant on harbours for the wealth derived from exports and imports. And there was a darker side to the coast, as the haunt of smugglers and of wreckers.

With all this activity, it is not surprising that the natural beauty of the coastline was largely ignored until the early nineteenth century. During the Napoleonic Wars, artists and writers – among them William Daniell – who were barred from Europe, turned their attention to the British Isles and began, almost for the first time, to appreciate the splendour of our countryside and coast. It was the moment to marvel at the achievements of the past, the harbours and fortifications, and to recognise the romantic appeal of the scenery. The splendour and terrors of the sea supplied further inspiration to artists and poets alike.

In Victorian times, fears of invasion were allayed and steam trains brought a new public to the coast: it was the beginning of the seaside holiday. Villages became tourist honey-pots, towns became resorts and the seaside became a mecca for leisure. With the tourist industry came a new threat to the coastline: building development.

From its founding in 1895, the National Trust has been dedicated to the preservation of the unspoilt beauties of Britain. Dinas Oleu (Gwynedd), our first property, was the start of our coastal acquisitions. In 1963, the Trust completed a survey of the coast and launched a national appeal to acquire as much as possible of our shoreline that remained unspoilt. "Enterprise Neptune", as the appeal was called, evoked an immediate and enthusiastic response; indeed, it has been our most successful fundraising campaign yet launched.

I welcome David Addey's record of the coast. We both take pleasure in the romance and beauty of this scenery. If the National Trust can take some credit for its preservation, we should remember that the accomplishment became possible through the support and gifts of those who have contributed to "Enterprise Neptune" with whom I join in welcoming this publication.

Lord Chorley
May 1994

PREFACE

It is nearly a quarter of a century since I first met David Addey. At that time he was a practising architect, with a small collection of English watercolours. A little later on, I don't remember exactly when, he invited me out to lunch, and to my surprise showed me a folio of his own watercolours. He told me he wanted to take up painting professionally – what did I think?

It was not long before architecture took second place, and was finally abandoned altogether. David had gone back to the great early traditions of British watercolour painting – topography, the depiction of the bones of a place without fuss or embroidery. There is a simplicity and directness about his watercolours that gives them a charm of their own. The many admirers of his work testify to this. Nowhere has this been more evident than in his annual sketching trips to the ports and estuaries of Northern France, where the French, wearying of post-post-impressionism, purchase practically the entire output of his exhibitions there.

Over the years the coast, waterways and old buildings of England, the sampans, junks and boatyards of the islands around Hong Kong, scenes in Washington D.C., and the south-west coast of Ireland, have all been the subject of his pencil. One day we were sitting in my office pondering his next move. The idea of following in the footsteps of an earlier artist's sketching tour suggested itself, and Hogarth and his friends' 'five days' peregrinations by land and water' to the Medway came to mind. Although the trip seems to have been a convivial one, only nine drawings were produced. David wanted a more substantial project, and in something less than a minute, we recalled William Daniell's epic 'Voyage Round Great Britain'; but this was mentioned almost in jest, since it took ten years to complete. Yet ports and coastal scenery are David's forte. It would be an enormous but challenging task, and it would be fascinating to compare today's views with those of the early nineteenth century. It would also provide subject matter for his pencil until the end of this century. The seed was sown. The challenge had to be met.

The first two stages of the voyage, completed in 1989 and 1990, culminated in successful exhibitions at my gallery in St James's; this volume is the outcome of those two years' work, and I hope that the success which this book deserves will ensure publication of future volumes, recording the completed 'Voyage Round Great Britain' by David Addey.

Martyn Gregory
(The Martyn Gregory Gallery)

INTRODUCTION

One of the most remarkable topographical books to be produced in the early years of the nineteenth century was 'A Voyage Round Great Britain' by the watercolourist and engraver, William Daniell, R.A. The book was published in eight volumes between 1815 and 1825, and the 308 beautifully engraved plates provide a fascinating record of the British coastline, its ports and harbours, lighthouses, ships and seafarers in the days of the Regency. The engravings are accompanied by a lively text which, in the first two volumes, was written by Daniell's companion, Richard Ayton, and in the remaining volumes by Daniell himself.

Daniell and Ayton set out from Land's End in 1813. They travelled north along the coast of England and Wales to Scotland, where Daniell was captivated by the rugged beauty of the dramatic scenery. Ayton left him at this stage and so Daniell continued along the east and south coasts of England until he arrived back at Land's End in September 1823. It had been intended to make the 'Voyage' by boat, hence the title, but early attempts at sailing off the north coast of Cornwall proved disastrous, and thereafter travel was made mostly on horseback, in a gig or on foot.

Born in Chertsey in 1769, Daniell showed an artistic talent from an early age and it was with his uncle, Thomas Daniell, that he received extensive instruction in painting and engraving. Thomas took a keen interest in the art of the aquatint, which was in the early stages of development and both he and William explored and used the medium to its fullest extent.

It was towards the close of the 18th century that the English were being fascinated by many aspects of the Orient, and by India in particular. With his love of travel and with a keen interest to see the wonders of that land, Thomas was granted permission in 1784 by the East India Company to work there as an engraver and to take William with him as his assistant. For ten years they travelled extensively, recording many scenes and enjoying or enduring many experiences. Soon after their return in 1794 they started work on their 'Oriental Scenery' – an enormous undertaking in six volumes, comprising a total of 144 coloured aquatints with an accompanying text. These volumes were published between 1795 and 1808. While working on this project William did not ignore his homeland and explored many areas of England and Wales, and London in particular. At this time he was also submitting his oil paintings to the Royal Academy, and was duly elected an associate in 1807. He had to wait until 1822 to be elected a full Academican against, of all people, John Constable.

With the experience gained on his travels in India, and having discovered the attractions of the English and Welsh countryside, it is not surprising that he had the idea of 'A Voyage Round Great Britain' and that such a project might bring just rewards.

My interest in the 'Voyage' was aroused when I was discussing with Martyn Gregory, the London fine art dealer, the possibility of embarking on another 'grand' project. Hitherto, among other things, I had produced a collection of 100 watercolours and drawings of the Thames for the David Messum Gallery in Beaconsfield, 110 pictures of Hong Kong for Martyn Gregory and 60 pictures of Washington D.C. for the Atlantic Gallery in Washington. I had enjoyed the challenge of these concentrated excursions over a period of ten years and, although in my earlier days as an artist I had thought of pursuing other subjects and other means of interpretation, it became clear to me that any satisfaction or success I might achieve lay in being a 20th century topographer. My training as an architect, and my long interest in the work of the 18th and 19th century watercolourists stood me in good stead; when I saw for the first time the nature of the 'Voyage' I realised that to depict the same views as they are today was another challenge that I could not resist.

The first task was to find the Daniell engravings from which to work: they would either have to be searched for and bought separately – a lengthy if not impossible, exercise – or I would have to purchase the set of eight volumes complete with the text. To my dismay, I discovered that these would cost something in the region of £18,000 to £20,000 for the complete set. The high price not only reflects the superb quality of the work but, sadly, the fact that many of the original volumes had been torn apart and the texts destroyed.

Fortunately the Tate Gallery had been able to purchase Daniell's original plates in 1972, and in 1978 a limited edition of 90 of each of the engravings was published, together with the complete text and illustrations in a smaller format in two volumes. At £80 this was a much more manageable price and so, armed with these as my reference, I began my 'Voyage'.

THE AQUATINTS (extracts from 'The Daniells' by Thomas Sutton)

Until towards the end of the 18th century, copper-plate engraving had been the method used to produce copies of original paintings and drawings. The development of the aquatint, which was introduced from the Continent by Paul Sandby (1725-1809), was especially successful in the imitation of the washes of watercolours with the effects of light and shade.

Although various materials can be used for the ground, Daniell employed copper for his aquatints of the Voyage. The plate is highly polished, coated with wax and then held in the smoke of a taper until the surface, having melted slowly, is an even, golden brown. The subject is then drawn or traced in reverse, with the pencil lines showing clearly against the hardened wax. The highest lights are 'stopped out' with an acid-resisting substance and the plate is then placed in a box containing thousands of particles of powdered resin. A current of air is then created, which causes the particles to rise and then settle like dust on the waxed surface of the plate. This is now placed in a bath of acid, which bites into the plate where the dust has disturbed the wax.

The plate is then removed, thoroughly rinsed, and the areas which have been sufficiently bitten are 'stopped out'. The process is repeated, the bitings becoming successively deeper, until the strongest darks are reached. The wax is then removed and the copper plate is seen to be pitted everywhere by minute holes, except where the stopping out has been used. The resultant print consists not of lines of varying depth or thickness, as in an etching or a copper-plate engraving, but of tones, similar to the washes of a watercolour.

The skilled engraver could lay his tones without etched outlines, though Daniell used the etched line for the masts and rigging of ships. Earlier aquatints were usually printed in a reddish-brown ink, but Daniell used at least two colours – warm grey and pale sepia, later adding a pale blue-grey. These colours were similar to the foundation washes used in watercolours of that period.

All the aquatints for the Voyage were made to the same size, 165mm by 237mm (6½″ × 9½″) with a 20mm (¾″) wide double lined surround incorporating the title of the subject in the bottom margin. The prints were hand coloured by trade colourists from notes provided by Daniell.

THE WATERCOLOURS

It is not my intention to describe the history or techniques of watercolour painting, as these subjects are covered adequately in many other publications, but a few details of the way I work may be of interest to the reader.

All subjects are drawn carefully in HB to 3B pencil. These are finished on the spot, with colour notes, on good quality watercolour paper of various weights and tones. The drawings are then coloured in my studio; for the smaller, detailed areas the paper is kept dry while the colours are applied, but for the larger areas, such as skies, it is worked on while slightly damp. My palette is generally limited, with the principal colours being Winsor blue, light red, raw sienna, yellow ochre and Payne's grey. Occasionally, I will use pastels, which help to enliven a sky, for example, that may have 'died' on me. The finished paintings vary in size from 165mm × 240mm (6½″ × 9½″) to 280mm × 410mm (11″ × 16″).

BIBLIOGRAPHY

Daniell, William — A Voyage Round Great Britain. The 1977 edition with notes, published by the Tate Gallery Publications Dept.

Drive Publications Ltd. — Illustrated Guide to Britain's Coast, The Reader's Digest Association Ltd, 1984

Kay, Alan — Corners of Old Margate, no. 65

Lucas, E. V. — Highways and Byways, West, Mid- and East Sussex, Macmillan and Co., 1937

Maxwell, Donald — Unknown Kent 1921, Unknown Sussex 1923, Unknown Dorset 1927, The Bodley Head.

Sale, Evans and McClean — Walking Britain's Coast – an aerial guide, Unwin Hyman Ltd., 1989

Somerville, Christopher — Coastal Walks in England and Wales, Grafton Books, 1988

Sutton, Thomas — The Daniells, Artists and Travellers, Theodore Brun, 1954

Woodward, Martin — Bembridge in old picture postcards, European Library

1 SHEERNESS

It is scarcely necessary to observe that the town of Sheerness has nothing very attractive within it and although a very unfavourable subject for the pencil, as a maritime station, it had too strong claims on the attention to be overlooked. The steam boats occasion a little bustle and animation, but the chief business is connected with the dockyard. Some temporary stir was observable at this time, arising from the presence of the king's yacht, and of the frigates destined to accompany His Majesty to Scotland. The tall building in the centre of the view is the steam engine and that to the right of it is the church in the churchyard.

1 SHEERNESS

It was 166 years after Daniell's visit here that I started on my 'Voyage'. Within a very short while gloom descended on me, and I almost began to wish that I had not embarked on such a venture. A clear, bright sky was quickly obscured by grey rainclouds accompanied by a brisk breeze. Worse still, there was no trace of Daniell's subject: the most likely viewpoint was a large fenced area of tarmacadam, suurrounded by high security fencing, all totally inaccessible. This was a depressing beginning and when I looked at the map of the British Isles on which I had marked all of Daniell's 308 subjects, it was with a heavy heart that I ended my first day. But something had to be recorded, and the nearest viewpoint was from the west side of the Medway; a start had been made, and there were now only 307 subjects to search for, besides views of my own – a possible total of 700 – 800.

2 THE RECULVERS

This important landmark is also known by the name of the Sister Churches, assigned to it in reference to the twin spires which crown the towers of the west front of the church. The abrupt bank of earth on which the church stands has been much wasted by the sea, and presents to view occasionally fragments of human bones, and other spoils of the cemetery.

2 RECULVER

From a distance, the haunting twin towers of Reculver appear to stand on their own, and it was thus that Daniell would have found them. Now they are surrounded by a large caravan park with the inevitable 'shanty town' of amusement arcades, gift shops, general stores and car parks. I have widened Daniell's view to include the public house. At some time between 1809 and 1819 the original spires blew down. In 1819 they were replaced, probably by Trinity House, with the skeleton towers depicted in Daniell's view. These may have been removed in about 1949. The towers were once called the Sisters of Reculver in commemoration of two sisters who were wrecked here. Both reached the shore safely but one died soon afterwards. The towers were regarded with such sanctity that no captain would sail past them without dipping his topsail in their honour.

3 MARGATE

Margate is too well known as a watering-place to need any description. Its noted promenade, the Pier, is introduced as a characteristic feature with the Tollhouse, where strangers, desirous of inhaling the sea breezes and looking at each other, pay two pence a day, or a penny each visit at their option. According to established usage the walking costume of a gentleman cannot be considered complete unless it includes a pair of tan-coloured shoes. Being situated at a convenient distance from the metropolis, and adapted to the expenses of the intermediate rather than the opulent classes of society, it has become the resort of a great number of citizens and their families and may be entitled one of the lungs of London.

3 MARGATE

Daniell's viewpoint still exists but the pier is partly obscured by the modern, tall, flat-roofed buildings of the lifeboat station and the yacht club. By now I had decided that to be too literal in my portrayal of the original views could, in some cases, lead to serious problems. The aspect depicted here is slightly lower than Daniell's and the main feature is the Harbour Company's Droit House. This is a replica of the original one built in 1830 which was bombed in 1942 and rebuilt in 1947. The Droit House is where the account books were kept. Almost every item entering Margate was charged a droit or tax. Unusual items listed were a corpse (10/6), a canary (6d), empty bottles (1d each). The pier was finished in 1815, just before the first paddle-steamers arrived with their hordes of trippers from London who swarmed over the sands and crammed the amusement arcades.

4 NORTH FORELAND LIGHTHOUSE

The principal feature of this view is the lighthouse, which is 63 feet high and stands on an eminence projecting into the sea in the form of a bastion. The elevation of its site, which is apparent from the circumstance of it overlooking the masts of the ships, renders it highly conducive to the safety of mariners especially in enabling them to avoid striking on the Goodwin Sands. The low houses that surround the light-house are the dwellings of the attendants who have it in charge. They have an air of loneliness, which at the time of this visit, was accidentally deepened into gloom by the approach of a hot-weather squall from sea-ward.

4 NORTH FORELAND LIGHTHOUSE

A light was exhibited on this cliff top in 1499 but the first real lighthouse was built in 1636. The lighthouse in Daniell's view was built in 1691 with two storeys being added in 1790. The present lighthouse is basically the same structure and is 85 feet to the top of the lantern. With the advent of satellite guidance for shipping, the life of the lighthouse could be drawing to a close as its function is being replaced by the thin, white aerial in the left-hand corner of my picture. A coastline without the comforting beams of a lighthouse is hard to imagine. A nearby housing development prevented me from finding Daniell's higher viewpoint.

5 BROADSTAIRS

Broadstairs is a quiet, comfortable retreat for those who, in retiring from town life to enjoy the salutary recreation of sea bathing, wish to avoid the noise and bustle of Ramsgate, or the gay frivolities of more fashionable watering places. If there be any drawbacks to the advantages and comforts of this secluded spot, it is that the chalk cliffs are so white as to be injurious to the eyes. Broadstairs was anciently called Bradstow of which its modern name is probably a mere corruption, or, in a nicer phrase, a fanciful refinement.

5 BROADSTAIRS

This is Charles Dickens territory; he first came to the town about 20 years after Daniell's visit in 1822. Bleak House, where he wrote 'David Copperfield', stands on the promontory in the middle distance of the picture. The viewpoint is identical to Daniell's, and I was greatly encouraged by the results of my efforts with a subject that had not been too spoilt by modern development and sea defences. My earlier gloom was beginning to lift and, as the weather was now becoming fine and warm, the prospect of, possibly, ten more years of exploring the British coastline began to take on a different aspect. Broadstairs still has the quiet, comfortable charm that Daniell found and, on a Sunday afternoon with a band playing in the bandstand, I found it almost too relaxing.

6 RAMSGATE

Ramsgate is no less noted as a watering-place of the genteeler class than as a haven of shelter for vessels when driven from their anchorage in the Downs by stress of weather. The tall structure in the form of an obelisk is a monument erected to commemorate the visit paid to this place by his present majesty on his progress to Hanover, when he was graciously pleased to declare Ramsgate a royal harbour. There are several good inns and elegant boarding houses; while the public libraries with their customary appendages, present some of the least exceptional means for dissipating that ennui which is generally recognised to be the endemic malady of a watering-place.

6 RAMSGATE

The obelisk featured in Daniell's view is still standing; the structure on the right is a lift shaft, which gives access to the shore from the upper promenade. The large building in the foreground is 'The Royal Victoria Pavilion', opened in 1904 by H. R. H. The Princess Louise. The cost was £21,962 10s 0d. The venue has been used as a concert-hall, dance-hall, variety theatre, and for bingo. It is now used as a Casino. Except for some neon lighting, the exterior of the building has remained unchanged since it was built.

7 DEAL CASTLE

Deal Castle is a fortress belonging to government and at the time of this visit, very few soldiers were stationed here, and there was an air of stillness, and a want of animation generally prevailing, which announced that this important station had been for some years reduced to the peace-establishment. The service allotted to the small garrison now occupying it may be considered as engaged almost exclusively in the prevention of smuggling. There is an establishment of pilots at Deal and connected with them there is a class of hardy and adventurous seamen called hovellers, who make it their particular business to succour vessels in distress and will often take the sea for this purpose in storms that would seem to baffle human skill.

7 DEAL CASTLE

Daniell's view shows the castle much nearer to the sea, whereas today there is a wide stretch of sloping shingle; there is no 'playground' for sandcastles, and this saved Deal from being overrun by Victorian holidaymakers. The greater part of the castle, which was built in 1540 by Henry VIII and laid out in the shape of a Tudor rose, has disappeared. The taller part of the structure on the right was built in 1802, but it received a direct hit in the Second World War and the castle was restored to its original Tudor appearance. A three-story block of flats has been built where the tower crane is shown.

8 WALMER CASTLE

Walmer Castle is situated at the commencement of the high ground which extends from hence, without interruption, to Dover; it commands a fine view of the Downs and of the coast of France. The level space observable in the foreground of the view is all shingle; and in hard blowing weather with very high tides, the whole of it, though very considerably above the level of high-water mark, is overflowed. The village of Walmer, called Walmer Street, contains some good houses, which, from their fine situation are inhabited by respectable families.

8 WALMER CASTLE

The escarpment referred to by Daniell is now covered with trees and shrubs and it is impossible to see the castle in the same way. Daniell shows a road running along the foot of the cliff and people walking over the shingle near the sea; it is just the same today, except that there is now a row of houses on the seaward side of the road. Deal pier, which was opened in 1957, can be seen in the middle distance, and the cliffs of Ramsgate are on the horizon. Walmer Castle, also built by Henry VIII to the same plan as Deal, is now the official residence of the Lord Warden of the Cinque Ports.

9 DOVER CASTLE

The view of Dover Castle exhibits that fortress as it appears to a beholder just after entering by the turnpike looking down upon the bay and the town. In its present state, this stronghold is justly designated as an immense congeries of almost every kind of fortification which the art of war has contrived to render a place impregnable; though its original importance, as a defence, has been materially diminished since the invention of gun-powder and the general use of canon.

9 DOVER CASTLE

This was the tenth day of my 'Voyage', and by now I realised that Daniell had taken considerable artistic licence with some of his views. One reason for this was that all his engravings were the same size, 165mm × 237mm, and in order to incorporate all that interested him and, possibly, to make his scenes more dramatic, he found it expedient sometimes to move things round. In this view the castle is a very dominant feature, and it is necessary to be much farther away from it in order to include the town and harbour. Dover is one of the original Cinque Ports, with Hastings, Sandwich, Hythe and Romney. Two others, Winchelsea and Rye, were added later. Their origin goes back to the Middle Ages, when they were designated the principal ports on the south coast which lie opposite France.

10 DOVER FROM SHAKESPEARE CLIFF

The view shows the exact position of the castle and includes that part of the town which extends to the pier. The new works constructed for the defence of the fortress consist of different batteries mounted with formidable artillery; casemates dug in the solid chalk rock, magazines, covered ways, various subterranean communications and apartments for soldiery.

10 DOVER FROM SHAKESPEARE CLIFF

A fine view of the town and harbour is obtained from this cliff, and the extent to which development has taken place at the 'Gateway to England' since Daniell's visit in 1823 is plain to see. In the foreground are the terrace houses of Aycliffe; and on top of the hill behind them is the Citadel which has been a prison since Napoleonic times and today is a Youth Custody Centre. The A20 now carves its way through Aycliffe, almost on the edge of the cliff and down into Dover. Towards the end of the Second World War a strange sight could be seen in the harbour. A large fleet was moored and preparing to set sail; but every ship was a dummy, carefully camouflaged to confuse the enemy and to distract attention from the planned landings on the beaches of Normandy.

11 SHAKESPEARE CLIFF

Though it cannot, strictly speaking, be ranked among the fashionable watering-places, Dover has become a favourite residence with many respectable families during the summer months. The prospects from various points in its vicinity are particularly romantic and interesting. One of the most noted of these is a cliff that rises abruptly from the sea, on the south-west of the harbour, to a height of about 270 feet. It has, by common consent, been denominated Shakespeare's Cliff, from the very obvious allusion to it in the tragedy of King Lear, where Gloucester, after having been deprived of sight, determines to throw himself into the sea from its summit.

11 SHAKESPEARE CLIFF

This massive chalk headland which rises to a height of over 90 metres, justly deserves to be associated with Shakespeare; it is the most monumental 'white cliff' of them all. On a distant cliff in Daniell's view you can see the church in Folkestone; my view is taken from farther back, so that I could incorporate the railway tunnel and the small cottage on the cliff top above the footbridge. This cottage, called 'Sunny Corner', was covered with posters proclaiming that it had survived Hitler's bombs and shells but that the Department of Transport was going to demolish it to make way for the A20. The owner, whose grandfather had built the cottage in 1875, fought a long campaign to save it but eventually it was compulsorily purchased and demolished in 1992. Its site now lies under the embankment of the A20.

12 FOLKESTONE

The town is built principally on the aclivity of a hill, on the summit of which and at the verge of the cliff, stands the church, a plain structure with a square tower which from its elevated and conspicuous position serves as a landmark. The handsome new houses on the heights attest to the growing importance of Folkestone as a watering-place. The eastern pier in its exposed position is liable to extensive injury in stormy weather and often requires to be repaired. Evidence exists in ancient records that gives reason to suppose that Folkestone was formerly of much larger extent and that it suffered at an early period from violent encroachments of the sea.

12 FOLKESTONE

Within 20 years of Daniell's visit to Folkestone the main railway line from London to Dover had been built, and a branch of it ran down to the harbour. This was taken right across the harbour on the brick arches shown in my view, and along the extended pier on the left to serve the cross-Channel ferries; these are no longer in service and the future of the harbour is undecided. The ferries may start again with more commercial traffic, or there may be a marina; the inner harbour might even be filled in and covered with houses and shops. The parish church of St Eanswythe is now dominated by multi-storey buildings, and there is a substantial promenade running under the East Cliff, which is much lower and more regular in shape. The large building beyond the brick arches is the Burston Hotel.

13 HYTHE

The churchyard, from its elevated site, commands a fine prospect of the sea and the coast of France. Seen from the point at which the present view was taken, the wooded ascent leading to it forms an agreeable coast feature, relieving, in some degrees, the formal effect produced by the Martello towers ranging at regular distances of a quarter of a mile from each other as far as the eye can reach.

13 HYTHE

Daniell's viewpoint is now submerged under a block of flats and, for the first time, I had to seek permission to enter an adjoining garden in order to obtain a similar view which, from this angle, is largely unchanged. An army firing range lies between the two Martello towers, and on the far horizon on the left Dungeness lighthouse and power station can be seen. The church of St Leonard is noted for its large, macabre pile of skulls and bones, said to be the remains of an invading army: being shorter and with differently shaped heads, they are unlike the bones of our buried ancestors.

14 DUNGENESS LIGHTHOUSE

In the view seen here the lighthouse is represented as seen during a thunder-storm; and this adventitious circumstance befel this building in 1822. On a Sunday morning it was struck by lightning so powerfully that the whole fabric, from top to nearly the bottom, was affected by the electric fluid. The inmates, alarmed at the instantaneous shock, and at the fall of bricks, mortar, dust and soot, hurried downstairs in the utmost trepidation. Scarcely had they gained the open air, when the keeper's wife recollected that her child had been left behind. She rushed upstairs almost frantic with apprehension. Entering the room she beheld the floor covered with rubbish; she approached the bed in an agony of despair – the babe lay there unharmed, and fast asleep!

14 DUNGENESS LIGHTHOUSE

The lighthouse in Daniell's view used to be in the centre of the circular white building, which accommodated the Trinity House staff. It was demolished in about 1904, when the one on the left in my drawing was built. This is now a museum, and the active lighthouse, which is on the right, was built in 1965. The sea has receded considerably along this stretch of coast, and in my picture the fishing boats can be seen in the distance. To the left of the lighthouse is the Dungeness station of the Romney, Hythe and Dymchurch miniature railway. You might think that I was sitting in solitary seclusion while painting this subject, but my back was against the security fencing of the Dungeness nuclear power station which looms dramatically out of the shingle.

15 RYE

Rye is a place of much bustle and is situated in a picturesque neighbourhood. It stands on an eminence on the west side of the Rother, of which the embouchere formed its harbour until the accumulation of sand rendered it almost unserviceable. To remedy this inconvenience it was determined to form a new harbour by cutting a large canal in a more direct line to the sea. Vessels of about two hundred tons are now enabled to come up to the quay on the north side of the town, about a mile and a half from the entrance. The low buildings seen on the left of the view are hot and cold baths erected since Rye grew into notice as a watering-place.

15 RYE

To obtain this view it was necessary to seek permission from the owner of a house on Point Hill, which rises up on the north side of the town. This was readily given and so, too, were sandwiches and coffee and, after I had nearly frozen to death, hot whisky. Daniell travelled mainly in the summer and, consequently, not one of his views shows trees without leaves. My preference is to work in the spring or autumn, chiefly because accommodation is easier to find and travelling is less fraught. When I first found this view of Rye it was virtually obscured by leaf-laden trees and I had to return to it a few months later. The saltings south of Rye were embanked in 1833 and up to that date the amount of land covered beneath the town depended on the state of the tide. The buildings referred to by Daniell as the baths could not have been seen from this viewpoint.

16 WINCHELSEA

Winchelsea derives all its interest from its antiquity and from the striking vicissitudes which it has undergone. It was one of the most powerful members of the Cinque Ports and contributed ten vessels to the fleet maintained by them for the public service. From facts recorded in history, there is reason to infer that its maritime force was not always employed for this laudable object, but was sometimes perverted by the ambition or cupidity of the people to enterprises of a most reprehensible nature.

The general aspect of the place is rather pleasant, and the ancient gate-way, through which the road passes, near the summit of the hill, has a romantic effect.

16 WINCHELSEA

This scene is virtually unchanged but Daniell has introduced Martello towers in the distance, which cannot be seen from this angle. The subject is still romantic, and the town itself, with so much history attached to it dating back to the 13th century, is a delightfully peaceful place in which to live or to explore. Old Winchelsea, which once stood in Rye Bay, was destroyed in a great storm in 1287, and the new town was rebuilt on higher ground with the church of St Thomas the Martyr in the centre. The town was repeatedly attacked by the French, who almost completely destroyed the church in the 15th century.

17 HASTINGS FROM EAST CLIFF

As a watering-place Hastings possesses the advantages of a salubrious air, a pleasantly secluded site and a peculiarly fine beach for bathing, together with many romantic walks and rides in its elevated vicinity. It occupies a site between two hills, that to the westward crowned with the ruins of an ancient castle and having a modern fort at its base. Beyond is seen Bexhill and in the extreme distance is the point of land called Beachy Head. Some boat-building is carried on here; and the fishery for herrings, as well as for soles, skate, mackerel, is pursued in the respective seasons, with great activity and success.

17 HASTINGS FROM EAST CLIFF

After a winter's hibernation I often visit Hastings and so it was natural that the 'Voyage' should resume here in March 1989. It was a cool, fresh day, but with the threat of rain by the afternoon. The depressing weather at the start of my 'Voyage' did not last for long and it is true to say that a day is rarely totally wasted. However, I always try to complete the drawing of a subject in one day, and it is therefore sometimes necessary to work quickly; this was the case with this view which, as well as presenting some difficult perspective, included a considerable amount of detail. The changes since Daniell's visit can be seen clearly, with the boating pool, leisure complex, and coach park in the foreground together with the lifeboat house, which is to be replaced in 1995. In the middle distance is the pier, built in 1872.

18 HASTINGS FROM NEAR THE WHITE ROCK

Beyond the town, along the beach near the difficult road to Bexhill, is the cliff called White Rock. The vicinity of Hastings, to the eastward is not without its attractions. As a residence the town itself is particularly agreeable presenting all the means of innocent recreation, which are suited to the demands of elegant society, unalloyed by those incentives to dissipation, which public places too commonly present. It is precisely the sort of summer retreat which persons would wish for, whose object is either the recovery or the preservation of health.

18 HASTINGS FROM NEAR THE WHITE ROCK

This very different interpretation of the view near the White Rock was taken from the pier and shows clearly how Daniell would foreshorten or condense his compositions. Ancient and modern Hastings meet at White Rock, which was cut back in 1834-35 to make way for the road to St Leonards. Inevitably, fish and chips is the popular meal today, and the large number of cafés is explained by the demand. The fishing fleet is still active and has been a source of material for many artists over the years. Under certain conditions, the light here is magnificent, and Turner considered his seascape of Hastings fishing boats, which he left to the National Gallery, to be one of his finest paintings and a challenge to a similar work by Claude.

19 NEAR BEACHY HEAD

Beachy Head is a headland forming the termination of that lofty hill, at the foot of which stands the village of East Bourne. In the view here given, a wreck is introduced, to show the position in which the Thames Indiaman was placed in January 1822 . . . the greater part of the cargo was saved and by the help of a steam vessel of eighty horses power, the fine ship was at length got afloat. The little building on the high ground is the signal station on Beachy Head. In the cliffs there are several large caverns said to have been cut by a clergyman who resided there, for the humane purpose of putting forth lights in stormy weather to guide unfortunate mariners to safety.

19 BEACHY HEAD

The name, Beachy Head, is derived from the Norman French, 'Beau Chef' and has nothing to do with the beach from which it rises to a height of over 150 metres – the highest cliff in the south of England. It was not until 1831 that the first lighthouse, the Belle Tout, was erected on top of the cliff; this was superseded in 1902 by the present lighthouse on the shore at the foot of the cliff, near Parson Darby's Hole. Parson Jonathan Darby from East Dean was the clergyman referred to in Daniell's text. An alternative version of the story is that he had the caverns hewn out for him to provide him with a refuge from Mrs Darby's tongue – or again, that they were used by smugglers. Inevitably there has been a great deal of erosion on this coastline, and Beachy Head itself is about 30 metres lower than at the time of Daniell's visit.

20 BRIGHTON

Brighton is the great point of attraction on the south coast and decidedly the most fashionable watering-place in the kingdom. It owes its distinction to the consistent patronage of his present majesty, who chose it as his favourite summer residence when it was in a comparative state of obscurity and under whose auspices it has risen, with a rapidity wholly unprecedented, to elegance and splendour.

To the left of the present view is seen the approach from London. The minarets in the central distance are those of the Pavilion; and the large dome, a little to the right, belongs to the stable of that palace.

20 BRIGHTON

Finding this view was like looking for a needle in a haystack and for some while I wandered round blocks of three-storey flats near the Ditchling Road: everywhere seemed to be inaccessible, but I was sure that one of the top floor flats would have the view I needed. Eventually, I knocked on a front door and my luck was in – and so, too, was a charming elderly lady who allowed me to make the drawing from her balcony.

The centre of the view is dominated by St Peter's Church, which was designed by Sir Charles Barrie and consecrated in 1828. Extensive development has taken place; the Pavilion is hidden behind the church and the dome is just visible. Although Daniell generally admired the work of John Nash, the architect of the Pavilion, his knowledge of Oriental design caused him to comment that 'there is not one feature, great or small, which at all accords with the purity, grandeur, and magnificence that characterises the genuine oriental style'.

21 NEAR REGENT'S SQUARE, BRIGHTON

This view is introduced for the purpose of exhibiting the style of architecture which has recently been introduced in the new buildings along the West Cliff. The houses are on a large and sumptuous scale, and, with their verandas and projecting balconies, partake as much of the Venetian character as is consistent with the climate of this country ... which is pronounced to be decidedly congenial to health and longevity; while a multitude of amusements, suited to the tastes and habits of a refined society are ever at hand, to dispel the 'taedium vitae', and give zest to existence.

21 NEAR REGENT'S SQUARE, BRIGHTON

Dawn, the time of day when a great deal of my work is started. It is also a time when you say 'hullo' to strangers who, more often than not, are exercising their limbs or their dogs; there seems to be a trusting camaraderie amongst early risers that slips away at about 7 o'clock. I sat in a promenade shelter to make this drawing and, unbeknown to me, two small boys had been peering over my shoulder. 'Gosh, mister', said one, 'I wish I could draw like that'. A compliment is always welcome; almost every line is still a struggle, and all I say to people who wish they could draw is, 'Have you tried? If not, just pick up a pencil and begin – and begin with something that interests you'.

This view is taken near Hove and shows the West Pier, which was built between 1863 and 1866, enlarged in 1893 but which, sadly, is now derelict.

22 SHOREHAM

Commonly called New Shoreham to distinguish it from a village of about 30 houses situated at the mouth of the Adur, New Shoreham is situated about half a mile lower down that river, on its east bank and has the advantage of a tolerably safe harbour, its entrance being formed by two projecting piers. It is a tide harbour; and, on account of its shifting sands, and a low flat rock, it cannot be entered except at high-water, when considerable animation is frequently given to the scene by the numerous coasting vessels arriving or departing. Its principal building is the church, which exhibits an interesting specimen of the union between Saxon and the early pointed style of architecture.

22 SHOREHAM

The church tower of St Mary de Haura is still a prominent feature in this view, which is from just below the footbridge that links New Shoreham with Shoreham Beach. Boats of all kinds are to be found here: old barges and torpedo-boats that now only move up and down with the tide – and sometimes don't even do that – yachts and motor cruisers, fishing boats and dinghies. For me, the life of a harbour is always fascinating; the changing tides, the smell of tar and mud, the decaying hulks covered with weed, the creaking of timbers; no wonder I have embarked on a project that has such an association with the harbours and coastline of the British Isles.

23 PIER AT LITTLEHAMPTON

This secluded and quiet spot is well suited to the taste of those who, in migrating to the coast for a season, wish to make as little variation as possible in their domestic habits and pursuits. The scenery around is rural, though it partakes but sparingly of the picturesque. The buildings for the accommodation of visitants are situated chiefly along the coast to the eastward of the scene here represented; they are built on a respectable scale, and their number will probably increase in proportion as the advantages of the place, with respect to comfort and economy, shall become more extensively known.

23 LITTLEHAMPTON

It was inevitable that sooner or later I would come across a view like this, and I pondered on the possibility of portraying it in moonlight or thick mist. But for posterity's sake, and to be true to the intention that my 'Voyage' should be a faithful record of the coast, I let the sun shine. Perhaps a three-masted schooner in full sail might have helped, but all that appeared was a small yacht. Littlehampton is not a paradise for artists but it certainly is for children, with its funfair on the east side of the harbour and its wide, sandy and safe beach on the west. It is also the end of almost 20 miles of coastal development from Rottingdean where, in many places, the villa- and bungalow-builders have been terribly busy.

24 VIEW FROM THE PARK, ARUNDEL

The magnificent castle of the Duke of Norfolk, though not strictly a coastal feature, commands a view of the sea and therefore comes within the fair scope of this work. The view here given includes a portion of the ground which is delightfully undulated with the profusely wooded bank, at the termination of which stands the castle. It would be needless to observe, that nothing more is here attempted than to convey a general idea of a scene presenting materials for an extensive series of views; the noble fabric of the castle, the woodlands and open grounds of the park, the groups of deer and the smiling landscape around, with the sea in the distance presenting a composition of the picturesque which might have enriched with new treasures even the imagination of a Claude.

24 VIEW FROM THE PARK, ARUNDEL

The woodlands that Daniell talked about were severely damaged in the hurricane of October 1987; while the Park has been re-planted, a few gaunt trees still remain as a reminder of that devastating night. Although the gatehouse and keep date from the 11th century, the greater part of the castle was built in Victorian times. My view shows the castle in silhouette from the north and, farther to the right, the top of the tower of the parish church and the short spire of the Roman Catholic cathedral. It is fascinating to conjecture on the origin of place names; is Arundel derived from 'Hirondelle', the name of the horse that belonged to Bevis the giant, or is it so called because of the river Arun running hard by?

25 BOGNOR

An elegant little bathing place which so lately as 1784 was known only as a fishing village and a resort for smugglers. Sir Richard Hotham, a hatter from London, determined to enjoy his well-earned fortune in retirement and erected here a summer residence. By subsequent purchase he became proprietor of the whole site of the village. Most of the houses adapted to the reception of visitors were also built by him on a plan so liberal and in so elegant a style, as to accord with his avowed intention of rendering Bognor the resort of select society. The view here given exhibits Selsea Bill in the middle distance. The building nearest the sea is the Library; and the larger house to the left is the principal inn of Bognor.

25 BOGNOR

The changes here have been considerable since Daniell's visit, but this was Daniell's viewpoint. The town still retains some of its earlier character, with very few buildings more than three storeys high. There are a number of pleasing Regency buildings, though some were demolished recently to make way for the Regis Entertainments Centre. This, in turn, may be torn down and replaced with a large bowling alley and cinema complex. Bognor, like Brighton and Worthing, enjoyed Royal patronage, and it was King George V who bestowed upon it the affix, Regis. A devastating storm in 1820 caused severe damage to the buildings depicted by Daniell and in 1823, as a result of the encroaching sea, the library was moved farther inland. The inn, incorrectly described by Daniell as being the building on the left, was destroyed by fire in 1826.

26 VIEW FROM PORTSDOWN HILL

For the purpose of delineating from one point a multitude of objects which could not be conveniently introduced in detail, an excursion was made to Portsdown Hill, a lofty and narrow ridge from whence was taken the annexed view, looking down on the harbour of Portsmouth. The aspect of that grand naval emporium, at this distance, is perhaps more impressive than any which it would exhibit to a beholder in its immediate vicinity. On the tongue of land to the right is Porchester Castle. Farther in the distance is Gosport backed by the Isle of Wight of which the portion here visible extends from Brading Harbour to near Ryde. In the harbour of Portsmouth are seen some objects strongly characteristic of a time of peace; they are ships laid up in ordinary.

26 PORTSMOUTH FROM PORTSDOWN HILL

By lining up the three promontories, I was able to find Daniell's exact viewpoint – just to the west of the Admiralty Research Establishment. Porchester Castle is in the middle distance on the right, but its aspect is not improved by the Vosper Thornycroft marine works in the foreground. Daniell refers to the ships in his view as 'being laid up in ordinary'. This phrase was used to describe ships stripped of all their rigging which, with guns, stores and other moveables, were taken on shore, the men and officers having all been paid off, except the boatswain, gunner, carpenter, cook, and six ordinary seamen, who remained on board.

My visit to Portsmouth in November 1989 brought to an end the first stage of my 'Voyage', the Isle of Wight having been explored in September that year.

27 WEST COWES

West Cowes is reputed to be the most pleasant and safe station of any on the British Coast for persons fond of aquatic amusements, because it is sheltered from all weather. It stands on a declivity of a steep eminence on the western side of the Medina, the largest stream of the isle; and as the houses seem ranged on terraces one above the other from the water's edge, it appears to great advantage, both from the sea, and from the opposite bank. The charm subsides on a nearer examination as the streets are narrow, irregular and ill built; a deformity which it perhaps owes to its sudden rise after the construction of a castle here by Henry the Eighth and to the want of concert among its first settlers, who were principally traders and fishermen, too much engrossed with their several avocations to attend to the elegancies of life.

27 WEST COWES

Cowes certainly continues to supply the 'aquatic amusements' praised by Daniell, and today, crammed with shipwrights' yards and yacht clubs, it is one of the world's greatest yachting centres. The Royal Yacht Squadron, housed in yet another of Henry VIII's fortresses, commands the harbour entrance, but in this view from the east bank of the Medina it is grossly overshadowed by a hideous block of flats built in the 1930s.

The architect, John Nash (1752-1835), built a castellated marine villa for himself in East Cowes, and Daniell, who remarked on its good taste, included it in his views. Regrettably it was demolished in c.1965 and in its place there is a large characterless housing estate which I just could not bring myself to put on paper.

28 LORD HENRY SEYMOUR'S CASTLE

The vegetation of the island is luxuriant and is enriched with a profusion of wild flowers of various kinds which, in their respective seasons of bloom, impart a gay and gladdening relief to the verdure. In short, the isle seems to have been formed and stored by nature to be a sort of pleasure garden for England, and in its culture and improvement the hand of art has been not sparingly or injudiciously exercised. An example presents itself of the success with which, in a very important part of its legitimate province, this improvement has been conducted. This is Norris Castle, better known as Lord Henry Seymour's Castle, having been built by the late James Wyatt Esq. Its site is very happily chosen and its style of architecture worthily accords with the scenery in which it forms so conspicuous a feature.

28 NORRIS CASTLE

PRIVATE, NO ENTRY, KEEP OUT, TRESPASS-ERS WILL BE PROSECUTED, are notices that are all too common in this land but Daniell makes no mention of such forbiddance on his travels. In my search for some of the subjects I may have to ignore these notices and hope for the best. Here, at Norris Castle, the signs were not at all welcoming, and I stood for some while pondering what to do. But there was no need to worry. Once the purpose of my visit had been explained, I was made most welcome. The castle has hardly changed since 1823, although Daniell's view is taken from a position that is now obscured by woodland. The castle was built in 1795, and Queen Victoria stayed here as a child before she built Osborne House in 1845-46.

29 RYDE

Ryde is the port of communication between the Isle of Wight and Portsmouth. The pier is of modern construction (1814) and has considerably improved the convenience of this place as a thoroughfare between the isle and the mainland; the beach here being of so gentle a slope that a boat cannot approach at low water within a hundred yards of the quay. A regulation is said to exist, under the sanction of an act of Parliament, by which any person, wanting to cross to Portsmouth, is empowered to command a boat to go off at any time of the tide on paying five shillings, the usual charge on the regular passage boat being one shilling.

29 RYDE

A busy, bustling town that was transformed in the mid-19th century from a small village into a major holiday resort after the construction of the pier depicted by Daniell. This pier, now one of three, was for foot passengers: the second pier was built subsequently for horse-drawn trams and, with the advent of the railways, a third pier was built in 1879. The regulation referred to by Daniell was modified over the years until it disappeared in the early 20th century. A boatman had to be licensed to provide this service and, if he failed to do so without just cause, he was liable to prosecution.

This was not a particularly enjoyable subject to attempt as the weather was unsettled and enthusiasm waned. In some cases it has been a help to have had the subjects chosen for me by Daniell, but in others I would rather have passed them by. On the other hand, with an extended project such as this, it is necessary to exercise a degree of discipline.

30 BRADING HARBOUR

The view of Brading Harbour is here seen from an elevated point on the neighbouring downs, which comprises the whole harbour with the town and church of Brading embosomed in wood; while in the distance appears a portion of the Sussex Coast terminated by Selsea Bill. The haven is an extensive tract of marshy ground, covered at every tide by the sea which enters through a narrow, shallow channel, navigable only for small vessels. The haven is a noted fishing ground for mullets, whiting, and flat fish; it produces excellent oysters and an abundance of fine cockles, the gathering of which affords employment to a great number of women and children in the summer season.

30 BRADING

It was while sitting here early one morning, and at exactly the same spot as Daniell, that I thought for a while about all the changes that have taken place over the last 166 years. Not only has nature played a part but man's achievements have been phenomenal. Imagine these views without the sound of cars or trains, no street lights or motor mowers, no pylons or telegraph poles, no aeroplanes or caravan parks, no radios or television sets. Your journey would have been on horseback, or in a gig, over muddy tracks; or at sea, with oar or sail.

The first attempts to reclaim the land at Brading Haven were made in 1620 but ten years later there was a serious breach of the embankment and the Haven reverted back to its original form. In 1878 a second attempt, despite a few problems, was eventually successful.

31 SHANKLIN CHINE

Shanklin Chine is a sort of gorge commencing near the village of Shanklin about half a mile from the shore and gradually increasing in dimensions until it opens upon the sea where it is nearly sixty yards wide and ninety deep. It is watered by a streamlet the banks of which abound in picturesque materials and their effect is heightened by the appearance of a few cottages, placed in striking positions. On one side is a neat little inn for the accommodation of tourists, who rarely quit the isle without paying at least one visit to this very celebrated spot.

31 SHANKLIN CHINE

It was necessary to return to this subject five years later as it had been totally obscured by foliage at the time of my first visit. The two cottages featured in Daniell's view still exist, although with considerable additions as they are now a public house, restaurant and gift shop. The word 'Chine' is derived from the Saxon 'cinan', meaning a crack. The most popular chines on the island are Shanklin, where there are remains of the Pipeline Under The Ocean (PLUTO) that was used to pump fuel to Normandy in the Second World War, and Blackgang, which was named after a local band of smugglers and is now a Fantasy Theme Park.

32 FRESHWATER BAY

On traversing the heights of Brook Down, which overlooks this bay, a squall of rain came on which, from its effect upon the skin of the face, might be truly called a sharp shower. The buildings on the right form that convenient and well-frequented receptacle for travellers called Freshwater Gate Inn. In the foreground, at a distance of a few yards from the shore, are two insulated rocks, through one of which the waves have wrought a perforation resembling a rustic arch.

32 FRESHWATER BAY

There has been little change to this scene, but Daniell has made the main headland, called Tennyson Down, appear to be much higher than it is. Lord Tennyson lived nearby at Farringdon House for nearly 40 years and walked over this down nearly every day.

The Freshwater Gate Inn, mentioned by Daniell, no longer exists. The large white building in my view is a Fellowship hotel and, to the left of this, on the headland, is the Redoubt fort built in the 1840s.

33 NEEDLES CLIFF AND NEEDLES

The Needles, which are really a very moderate height and destitute of any affinity with their name, appear diminutive and insignificant. Their substance being chalk, they are continually lessening in dimensions, but are nevertheless dangerous in blowing and foggy weather. They owe their appellation to a lofty pointed rock whose summit was 120 feet above high water mark, and being extremely slender in proportion to its altitude, it might, when seen from afar, be likened, with a little pardonable extravagance by hyperbole, to the implement of which it bore the name. About sixty years ago, having been undermined by the sea, it fell with a tremendous crash, and the concussion was perceptible, according to some accounts, at a considerable distance.

33 THE NEEDLES

The 'lofty pointed rock' mentioned by Daniell was called Lot's Wife and collapsed in 1764. The remaining rocks appear to be less jagged than in his view. The lighthouse at the tip was built in 1859.

My four day tour of the island with my wife finished here on 12th September 1989. Our base had been a small bed and breakfast in Brading, from which we made daily excursions to the various viewpoints; we found the island pleasantly relaxing. Daniell spent five days on his tour of the island in September 1822, and his return journey from Cowes to Lymington on the 9th September took three hours on a smooth sea; ours from Fishbourne to Portsmouth took rather less.

34 CHRISTCHURCH

The priory was founded in Saxon times and subsequently rebuilt in later years on an extensive and superb scale. According to monkish legend, this pious undertaking was favoured with celestial aid. During the hours of labour a supernumerary workman was observed among the people employed, though at the times of refreshment, or for wages, only the stated number appeared. When the fabric was advancing to its completion, it happened that a large beam was found to be too short. As no remedy could be devised the disconcerted workmen retired home. On their return next morning they were surprised to find the beam in place lengthened out a full foot beyond the required dimension. Amazed at the miracle, they recollected the mysterious stranger, and there was only one opinion as to who it might be.

34 CHRISTCHURCH

June 17th 1990 marked the start of the second leg of my 'Voyage' but the after-effects of a late night persisted well on into the day, and the long drive from Sussex to Dorset, with no accommodation reserved at the end of it, did nothing to lift my spirits. But my luck was in, and when I arrived at Christchurch I found both the subject and a comfortable bed and breakfast almost immediately. Thus encouraged, I set to work straight away. In the left foreground of Daniell's view there is a small boat; this is the foot-passenger ferry across the river Stour which is still in service today. Also, on the right, is the 11th century Place Mill, which is contemporary with the priory and was used for milling flour. Daniell's reference to the Monkish legend is interesting: a similar miracle is said to have occurred at a nunnery in Folkestone about 600 A.D.

35 POOLE HARBOUR

Poole is a clean little town, seated on the north side of the bay to which it owes its name, its site being a peninsula, joined by a narrow isthmus to the mainland, which, in this vicinity, is a bleak and desolate heath. The town employs many vessels in the Newfoundland fishery and in the coasting trade. The public buildings are the market house, the town hall and the wool-house, none of which can be said to possess much architectural beauty. The church is a small fabric of some antiquity. In the view here given it is to be observed, that on the conical eminence on the left, in the distance beyond the harbour, are situated the ruins of Corfe Castle.

35 POOLE HARBOUR

It was six o'clock in the morning when I started on this watercolour; the sky was remarkably clear and there was total silence as I contemplated the scene from Constitution Hill. There has been an immense amount of development since Daniell's day when there appeared to be just a church and barely a dozen other buildings: those referred to by Daniell as not possessing 'much architectural beauty' still exist and are listed as of special architectural or historical interest. The wool-house or Town Cellars is Listed Grade I, and incorporated in the Waterfront Museum Complex. The market house was below the town hall, now known as the Guildhall, and is Listed Grade II* – how the passage of time makes us see things differently.

36 CORFE CASTLE

This grand and imposing ruin, though not strictly a coast feature, had a claim on the pencil which it was impossible to resist; and if the reader cannot dispense with an apology for its appearance in this series, he must understand that there is a hill to the westward from which the sea can be distinctly seen.

The castle itself was one of the strongest and most ancient in the kingdom and from the condition of its ruins, the beholder is naturally led to imagine that great labour must have been employed in its destruction. This event took place in 1646 when the walls were partly overthrown, and partly blown up with gunpowder.

36 CORFE CASTLE

Daniell remarks that although Corfe Castle is not strictly a coastal feature, it is possible to see the sea from the hill to the west of the castle. He said the same about Arundel Castle; if he had adopted this policy too often he would never have finished his 'Voyage'. The bridge shown in this view is much farther to the right and links the main gate of the castle with the village. On the left, in my view, is a railway bridge, which, though disused at the moment, may yet carry steam trains from Swanage to Wareham. The castle was the model for Corvesgate Castle in Thomas Hardy's Wessex novels.

37 SWANAGE

Swanage is a place now noted for its quarries, and formerly for a material called Purbeck marble, with which the hall at Winchester, and the columns in Salisbury cathedral, are said to have been constructed. It stands in a low site on the margin of a bay, bounded on the south by a spit of land called Peveril Point. The comforts and advantages of cleanliness do not seem to be very highly appreciated in Swanage, with the very important exception of its principal inn, The Ship, which is kept in admirable order and affords accommodation to the traveller at very reasonable charges.

37 SWANAGE

I reached Swanage after a wet and miserable day. On occasions like this one has to summon up all one's will power and determination to sit down and paint. The pier depicted in my painting was built in 1896 for £10,000 and although derelict at present, plans are under way for its repair and refurbishment. Behind this pier are the remains of another pier which was built in 1859 and used for shipping the local stone. In 1874 a steamer service was started but the trippers who landed on the pier must have wondered what sort of place they had come to, as the whole structure trembled like a spider's web. It fell into disuse in the 1920's. The Ship Inn, mentioned by Daniell, still exists. At the foot of Foreland Point in the distance, stand the chalk pinnacles of Old Harry and Old Harry's Wife, both of which have suffered considerable erosion since Daniell's visit.

38 LULWORTH COVE

Lulworth Cove is entered from the sea through a wide rent in the cliff, and is bounded on either side by high, rugged rocks, those towards the opening corresponding with each other in the texture and direction of their strata. In the western range are some large and grotesque caverns, formed by the continued action of the waves, which have considerably increased the extent and depth of the cove within the remembrance of several natives of the village. It seems to have been the resort for smugglers, as there is a station on the neighbouring hill for men engaged in the preventive service.

38 LULWORTH COVE

This view has hardly changed, but the cove has become one of the most famous coastal features in Britain. Never go there on a summer week-end, when it becomes a vast annexe to the Motor Show on a Bank Holiday. There are times when I envy Daniell and the period in which he travelled; he had his difficulties, but as he would have had little idea of future 'progress' he would not have known what he was missing.

39 WEYMOUTH

Weymouth is situated along the shore of a fine bay near the mouth of the little Wey. The esplanade, which was originally a sort of mound formed by successive accumulations of the rubbish of the town, is now one of the finest marine walks in England. The sands are smooth and firm, and the waters of the bay so well screened by the surrounding hills as to be comparatively tranquil even in boisterous weather. The air is particularly salubrious; and the various places of note in the environs offer the most agreeable incentive to exercise, either in a short or a lengthened excursion.

39 WEYMOUTH

The foreground in Daniell's view is now a yacht club, and the fine Georgian character of the seafront still remains largely unspoilt. The only eyesore appears to be the back of a well-known store that I have just managed to conceal behind the buildings on the left. To the right, but outside the picture, there is a large theatre that rather dominates the scene. George III visited Weymouth in 1789 and was the first monarch to use a bathing machine. In so doing, he made the town a fashionable resort for his fellow Georgians. It was here that I nearly had a disastrous bed and breakfast where, I was told afterwards, even the cost of teabags would have been added to my bill.

40 LIGHTHOUSE, ISLE OF PORTLAND

This is the Lower or New House, which was erected in 1789 at the expense of the Trinity Corporation. The distance of the lighthouse from the cliff is 1608 feet, as appears from an inscription over the doorway, over which it is recorded that the founders erected this building 'for the direction and comfort of navigators, the benefit and security of commerce, and a lasting memorial of British hospitality to all nations'. Large masses of sunken rock extend in a south-westerly direction to a considerable distance from the shore, and eastwards as far as St Aldhelm's Head; and the difficulty of navigating this part of the channel is augmented by that perilous surf called the Race of Portland.

40 LIGHTHOUSE, ISLE OF PORTLAND

Of the two old lighthouses at the southern end of the island, nobody seemed to know that this was the one that Daniell had depicted – not even the lady who lived in it and who thought this view was of one lower down. She told me she was an artist but was not in the least bit interested when I replied that I was one too – perhaps she was too busy.

In his text Daniell refers to the Lower or New House but it seems to me that he has depicted the old high lighthouse. It is not surprising, therefore, that there was some confusion in identification. Both lighthouses were replaced in 1869 and remained in use until the present Portland Bill lighthouse was built in 1906. It is the old high lighthouse that I have shown in my view.

41 ST CATHERINE'S CHAPEL, ABBOTSBURY

The area of this small but curious ruin is eighteen paces by nine. The material is a reddish stone, dug from the hill, and apparently too soft a nature to offer due resistance to the weather; yet considering its exposed site, the chapel is in a tolerable state of preservation. It was built about the time of Edward the Fourth, probably in expiation of the crimes committed during the long and sanguinary war of the Roses. From its lofty situation, the chapel serves both as a land and sea mark; and in times of war it may also have answered the purpose of an observatory, from whence to watch the motions of the hostile navies that so frequently infested this coast.

41 ST CATHERINE'S CHAPEL, ABBOTSBURY

This small but robust chapel stands alone on Chapel Hill to the south of Abbotsbury and is a subject where Daniell allowed himself considerable artistic licence. By no stretch of the imagination can you see Chesil Bank and the Isle of Portland while at the same time looking up at the chapel. In his views it was not so much his intention to be accurate as to show other features in a given area. Elsewhere he moves rocks, lighthouses, headlands and mountain ranges, which would otherwise be outside the line of vision and thus create double perspectives. The chapel is no longer in use, but in times past the spinsters of Abbotsbury, as they climbed the hill, prayed to their patron saint for a handsome, rich husband – soon!

42 BRIDPORT HARBOUR

Bridport harbour, at the time of this visit, appeared to be in a deplorable state, the entrance being choked up with sand. There were many vessels in it, and two or three on the stocks, of the smaller class of course, as this is a tide-harbour, accessible only at high water. The coast in this vicinity may be considered picturesque, as the white cliffs, rising precipitately from the sea, possess great variety of form.

42 BRIDPORT HARBOUR

It was too windy for me to climb up the hillside to Daniell's viewpoint so I took shelter lower down behind a fence. The harbour is now busy with a few fishing boats and many pleasure craft and, after I had finished my sketch, I spent some time watching the activities round the public launching ramp. After a while an immaculate Range Rover, towing an equally immaculate motor launch, was driven imperiously into position and proceeded to back down the ramp. It stopped, and the driver climbed out to see that all was well; but because the tide was at its highest, it concealed the extensive slippery green weed on the ramp. Silently and remorselessly, vehicle and boat slowly slid into the water and disappeared. There was great consternation – and much laughter.

43 LYME REGIS FROM CHARMOUTH

Lyme Regis is situated in a declivity near the sea almost contiguous to the boundary which separates Dorset from Devon. The labouring classes which inhabit it derive their principal subsistence from the sea, and their occupation is designated by the fishing boats and lobster-traps seen in the foreground. The object resembling a pier, seen in the distance, is that unique breakwater called the Cobb, which was originally composed of vast pieces of rock rudely piled upon each other, but is now formed of stone compacted with cement. It is of very great importance on this part of the coast, there being no other shelter between Start Point and the Road of Portland as it affords perfect security from the violence of south-west gales.

43 LYME REGIS FROM CHARMOUTH

I visited Charmouth the day after West Bay, and by now the strong wind had developed into a gale with heavy showers. Daniell's viewpoint was taken from near the building on the right of my picture, but I wanted to include this so I made my way to a caravan at the foot of the cliffs to find some shelter. This turned out to be a beach café and appeared to be closed, but I had just started my sketch when the door flew open and out came a welcome mug of tea. The wheel-tracks in the sand were made by a vehicle that had come to collect a large fossil – greatly to the indignation of the inhabitants of the caravan who said it was illegal to do this.

44 SIDMOUTH

Sidmouth has no very eminent advantages for sea-bathing, but the air is reputed to be as mild and as salubrious as that of Italy, and therefore favourable for invalids who are subject to disorders of the lungs. For the recreation of visitants, there are two circulating libraries, furnished with fresh novels for the season, as well as a daily supply of lighter fare for those who with Dr. Johnson are disposed to wonder how any man can exist without a newspaper. The situation of the town is interesting, the country around it is abundantly clothed with trees of the finest growth and presents, in diversified modes of composition, the three main elements of the picturesque – rock, wood, and water.

44 SIDMOUTH

I wanted to paint this view with the sun behind me so I had to make an early start. It was a long climb up Salcombe Hill in search of Daniell's viewpoint; it needed to be seen shortly after dawn so I had left my bed and breakfast at 6.00 a.m. I settled down to begin my sketch only to find that my pencils were still in the car. So back down again – 40 minutes wasted. Later, and worse still, I discovered on my return to my lodgings that I had selected the wrong view. Once I had recovered from my stupidity, I returned and found the right place inland. The town retains much of its Georgian and Regency charm and in portraying the scene as it is today I have endeavoured to create the feeling of a Daniell aquatint with colour washes applied over a monochrome background.

45 EXMOUTH

Exmouth has little to commend it at present, but the improvements which are in contemplation will doubtless render it a desirable residence. The high ground, where some of the principal lodging houses are situated is called The Beacon. On the morning after arriving here, the entrance of the river presented an animated scene. It blew fresh from the north and east, and a pilot worked down to the outlet between the sands, to conduct two sloops into the harbour. The sea running on the edge of the sands was one sheet of white foam, and the vessels, under close-reefed topsails, were tossed about in a spirited manner, but by following their guide they effected their passage into the river, and were soon in smooth water.

45 EXMOUTH

After a wretched bed and breakfast in Lyme Regis, which might well have been run by a former regimental sergeant-major -'breakfast is at 8.30 sharp' – it was a pleasure to find one in Exmouth that was a complete contrast and I stayed there for several nights. To find Daniell's viewpoint it was necessary to thread one's way through some housing estates and then walk along the edge of the cliffs. Rain threatened, so a rapid start was necessary but progress was impeded by the discovery of an escaped budgerigar. So, back to the houses in search of its owner; but I had no success, and eventually the local constabulary took charge of the little creature. The view, from Orcombe Point, shows Holy Trinity Church, and the row of houses depicted by Daniell and called The Beacon, still exists. Lady Nelson and Lady Byron lived in two of these residences.

46 TEIGNMOUTH

During the bathing season Teignmouth is the resort of much company. There is a smooth, sandy beach with a very gentle slope to the sea, for those who choose to perform their ablutions with the aid of vehicles, commonly or rather oddly called machines; and a range of hot baths has been attached to the principal hotel, for the benefit of invalids. The public libraries and reading rooms are well supplied with newspapers; but these prove but a precarious comfort to idlers in a time when it is so frequently happens there is 'no news'. The cliffs that face the sea are from seventy to eighty feet in height, and consist of sandstone, of which the deep red hue forms a strong contrast with the few patches of verdure upon them.

46 TEIGNMOUTH

After going up and down and in and out of numerous roads and pathways, I eventually found Daniell's view but not before 'rescuing' a lady who had managed to reverse her car up a steep bank into a private garden. After much tugging and pushing, levering and humping, the car was eventually returned to its customary environment.

The church is now more prominent, but the building on the right, which is a school for the blind, is totally obscured by trees. On the hill on the opposite side of the river is a modern building which constitutes a most unsympathetic intrusion into the rolling landscape – not a good example of planning control.

47 BABICOMBE

This romantic little watering place is deservedly a favourite with those who prefer true seclusion to the questionable delights of merely fashionable retirement; and many families may be said to domesticate here during the season. The genteel cottages (if such a term be admissable) which are so numerous in the neighbourhood, afford abundant evidence of this fact; but though they doubtless combine elegance with comfort, they are in too ornate a style, and have too much prettiness about them to accord with the general character of the scenery. Their number seems likely to increase, for Babicombe must ever continue to be exclusively a watering place, as it has no harbour, and the few fishing boats which it can maintain will find sufficient employment in the service of visitants.

47 BABBACOMBE

This 'little watering place' is, in fact, Oddicombe Beach and can be approached either by a cliff railway which terminates in the blue and white building on the left, or by a 1 in 3 hill. I was rather discouraged by the subject as it unfolded itself, but the job had to be done, and the significant changes will be noted; the rocks in the foreground of Daniell's view have disappeared. Normally, I make my excursions in the spring or autumn, but it was mid-August when I was exploring this stretch of the coast – the busiest time possible. Nevertheless it was enjoyable, the weather was fine and everybody seemed to be happy . . . except that the situation in the Gulf was becoming serious.

48 TORR ABBEY, TORQUAY

Torquay is one of the most important of those maritime stations which have been formed by nature on the south coast of Great Britain for the purpose of enabling her to acquire and to maintain the empire of the seas. Torr Abbey, the distant subject in this view, which is taken from the terrace above the quay, is another modernised antique. The mansion, which is founded on the arches of the antique structure, consists of a centre and two wings, one of which is connected with a castellated gateway, having octagonal towers and battlements. The grounds are adorned with fine trees forming noble avenues, and the walk from Torquay, through the wood, forms a very romantic approach to the abbey.

48 TORRE ABBEY, TORQUAY

To be confronted with a scene like this can be very disheartening, all the more so when you compare it with Daniell's view. The abbey is somewhere in the distance, and barely visible behind dense foliage; it is now an art gallery. The small curved jetty still exists but much land has been reclaimed behind it on which a fine pavilion was built in 1912. This is now a general market hall, but unfortunately its appearance from the harbour has been spoilt by a two-storey car park.

49 BRIXHAM

Brixham is inhabited principally by fishermen, and has a small pier for the accommodation of vessels. Of these there was a considerable number in the harbour, which, like that of Torquay, is dry at low water, and consequently emits a scent by no means agreeable to mere landsmen. The fishing vessels belonging to Brixham are said to amount to at least 100 sail. Some of them are built much larger than those of former times, and in the summer months are engaged in the culm trade, the average burthen of each being eighty quarters by Winchester measure, which is sixteen heaped bushels to the quarter.

49 BRIXHAM

This was a most enjoyable subject to draw but it took a long time. I sat on some waste land very close to Daniell's viewpoint. The smells he commented on were not so noticeable, but the screeching of the seagulls became almost unbearable. The small quay is little changed but the large one has been extended, and a new quay with substantial warehouses was built in the 1970s to cater for the thriving fishing industry. The 'culm trade' Daniell refers to is the transport of coal-dust.

It has been my good fortune to meet many people who not only stop to have a chat but provide me with information, refreshment, or accommodation. So it was here, and I was invited into a nearby house for tea which, at the end of an exhausting day, was most welcome.

50 ENTRANCE TO DARTMOUTH

The church on the hill in the distance belongs to the town, while on the right, which is the Kingswear side, stands the ancient castle, which is so exposed to the sea, that the spray often beats over it in stormy weather. The prospect of the river, from any part of this bank, is eminently beautiful, and comprehends all the essential ingredients of landscape, wooded hills, buildings, rocks, and water; so disposed and blended as to produce the happiest effect. On the point where the Castle and St Petroch's Church are situated there stood not long ago a few noble trees, which, by order of some modern Goth, have been cut down.

50 ENTRANCE TO DARTMOUTH

There are times when I wish I had done my homework more thoroughly instead of relying on my memory; this was one of those occasions. A quick glance at the map; not far to go; just time to finish a drawing before sunset. But no, it was a long walk, up and down, and no sign of the subject; a few things were said under my breath about a certain Mr Daniell. Suddenly, quite by chance, I came across a small clearing that gave access through dense undergrowth to the water's edge, and there, straight in front of me, was the view. Details have changed, but the general appearance is similar, although, once again, Daniell has greatly exaggerated the height of the hills.

Kingswear Castle, on the right, was built about 1491 and Dartmouth Castle on the left, was completed in 1494.

51 THE JUNCTION OF THE DART WITH THE SEA

It is thought proper to introduce another view of Dartmouth, including the junction of the river with the sea and presenting a very fine combination of wood and rock. In the appearance of the town there is one peculiarity which a stranger cannot fail to remark; its prevailing colour of grey, from the abundance of slate; and the inhabitants, with praiseworthy unanimity, have imparted to the exterior of their walls the same sober tint, so that the houses here seem to wear the local livery of nature. A considerable portion of the trade of Dartmouth arises from the Newfoundland fishery, in which it is said to employ nearly 3000 men. The merchants engaged in this trade reside principally in a spacious street near the quay. In this harbour, as in Torbay, many of the vessels have tanned sails, of a red tinge, derived from the oak-bark used in the process, which is said to render them much more endurable.

51 THE JUNCTION OF THE DART WITH THE SEA

The harbour entrance is much narrower than Daniell has depicted it, and the rocks and trees in the foreground have been replaced by houses and roads. The spire on the 17th century church of St. Petrox was removed in 1856. While searching for this view I approached a local inhabitant to seek his opinion; after a brief conversation, we parted. I was then invited into a house nearby where I was able to sit in comfort and, fortified with tea and cake, set about my task. About three weeks later I received a letter from the inhabitant who, while visiting the same house, discovered that we had known each other about 30 years before; neither had recognised the other at our brief meeting.

52 NEAR KINGSWEAR ON THE DART

This view was selected as an instance of the beautiful situations in which the houses are built on this river. Most of them are so placed as to command highly interesting prospects of those banks which they may be truly said to adorn, and have that air of comfort and elegance which ought to prevail in a residence destined solely for retirement. The villas that overlook the Dart are adapted for the residence of the affluent and this is one of the pleasantest of them. It appears, as seen in this view, to be almost insulated on its rocky site, but it has a very good carriage road to the town of Kingswear, and there is a flight of steps to the river's bank, for the convenience of a water excursion.

52 NEAR KINGSWEAR ON THE DART

On a number of occasions I have had to seek permission to enter private gardens in order to reach Daniell's view. This was one of them, and I found the owner busily attending to one of his boats in the garage. Without hesitation I was immediately taken down to the waterfront, where this delightful view presented itself. The house depicted by Daniell might have been in one 'of the beautiful situations' but it fell into the sea some years ago. The remains of the flight of steps can be seen in the bottom right-hand corner of my picture.

Afterwards I was invited to stay the night, and a mutual interest in watercolours led to an enjoyable evening's discussion.

53 KINGSWEAR

Kingswear is represented as seen when looking from Dartmouth towards St. Petroch's Church and the Castle. It is surrounded by lovely scenery, and commands a very fine prospect of the entrance of the river, which at this time was enlivened by the presence of numerous vessels, some working in, and others working out of the harbour, under a gentle breeze. From the composition of its name, the town may have owed its origin to some sovereign, whose title, however, has not been distinctly specified.

53 KINGSWEAR

Basically this scene is very much the same, except for the increase in the number of houses on the hillside. The end of a carriage on the Paignton and Dartmouth Steam Railway can be seen on the left, together with the passenger-and-car ferries. The church of St Thomas à Becket dates from 1175 when Kingswear was one of the first stops for pilgrims travelling from France to Canterbury. Its tower appears to be shorter now than in Daniell's view but the main body of the church was rebuilt and increased in height in 1847. King John is believed to have owned land near a small creek on the east side of the Dart, on which stood a mill with a weir; hence, the probable origin of the name 'Kingswear'.

There is still great charm in the Dart Valley, and development has been carefully controlled. Like Daniell, I 'quitted these interesting shores with reluctance'.

54 SALCOMBE

There is a natural breakwater with a channel on each side, and the little town of Salcombe is situated just round the point. The bank, extending from thence to the mouth of the river, is most beautifully wooded. The shore is rocky, and on one of its most striking points stands Woodville, the seat of Mr. Yates, commanding a delightful view towards the sea. So genial is the climate in this sheltered place, that his gardens produce oranges and lemons, and fruits of the choicest kind are in abundance. On the verge of the grounds of Woodville, there is a little cove, where Mr. Yates contrived a secure place for the preservation of fish; but notwithstanding all his efforts for their safety, the sea otter constantly destroyed them.

54 SALCOMBE

It was difficult to locate this scene accurately but perhaps Daniell was in a boat. He refers to the house depicted as 'Woodville' but the present house, called 'Woodcot of Woodville', bears no resemblance to the one in his view, except for the castellated steps on the left-hand side. These are unrelated to the structure on which I sat; this appears to have been a fortification built to repel Napoleon and subsequently used as a gun emplacement in the Second World War. The arrival of the Brixham trawler 'Providence', was a welcome sight, and a small reminder of the flavour of days gone by.

In 1944 thousands of Americans embarked from Salcombe, to play their part in the D-Day landings in Normandy.

55 BOVISAND

Bovisand is a secluded village on a bay of that name. At a short distance from it, in a hollow between two hills, has been formed a noble reservoir of fresh water, supplied from an excellent stream, and capable of containing from ten to twelve thousand tons; a quantity for fifty sail of the line. The water is conducted through iron pipes to Staddon Point, where a quay has been commenced, which, when complete, will be furnished with all the apparatus necessary for supplying the ships in the most expeditious manner. The estimated expense of the undertaking is £16,000; but the advantages that will accrue to the British navy from so essential a resource, on urgent occasions, are incalculable.

55 BOVISAND

This scene is much the same today but there is a caravan park between the house and the sea. The small hut on the right-hand hill still stands, so does the main part of the house, even to the urns on the parapets. It was not possible to obtain the same view because of dense woodland, so I have taken mine lower down and omitted the house, which occupied too much of the foreground.

Difficulties were encountered with two goats, one of which proceeded to eat my drawing board while the other practised its head-butting technique on me.

56 QUAY AT STADDON POINT, PLYMOUTH

This quay has been erected for the convenience of boats taking water for vessels in the Sound. At the time of the present visit, this useful work was in progress; and the large blocks of stone lying near it manifested the strength of the structure. It will afford a safe shelter for boats in boisterous weather.

56 STADDON QUAY

The basic shape of the quay has not been altered since it was built in 1823. Since 1970 the quay, together with the 19th century fort alongside, has been used by the Fort Bovisand Underwater Centre. At anchor in Plymouth Sound was the Royal Fleet Auxilliary, 'Fort Grange', which sailed for the Gulf the next day.

After my visit to Staddon Quay I stayed for a night at a public house in Turnchapel. There I fell into conversation with one of the customers who expressed great interest in my project; he was a jovial little fellow, an ex-Shell tanker bosun who, without more ado, whisked me off to Plymouth where we visited six pubs, two of his friends, and the army guards at the Citadel — none of whom seemed the least bit pleased to see him.

57 THE CITADEL, PLYMOUTH

The citadel is situated on the extremity of the Hoe and it was erected in the reign of Charles the Second, on the site of a fort built by Elizabeth; and consists of three regular and two irregular bastions, the curtains of the former being strengthened by ravelins and hornworks. On the east, north and west sides, are a deep ditch, counterscarp, and covered way, palisadoed. In time of war the parapets are mounted with a great number of cannon, and there is a garrison consisting of several companies of invalids. The prospects from this fortress are varied and delightful and that which is here selected is to the eastward and includes the entrance of the Catwater, with the tower of Mount Batten on the right.

57 THE CITADEL, PLYMOUTH

Basically the scene is little changed, except that there is now a road in front of the Citadel with a conveniently placed public seat close to Daniell's viewpoint. The curtains referred to by Daniell are the ramparts between the bastions. Ravelins are detached works with two embankments raised before the side of the ditch nearest the besiegers; hornworks are demibastions joined by a curtain; palisadoed means surrounded with stakes – useful information for architectural scholars. Daniell gained access to the Citadel to record two other views but I was unable to do so, probably as a result of the visit the night before.

58 VIEW FROM MOUNT EDGECUMBE

The view from Mount Edgecumbe, which includes the Breakwater and the Mewstone Rock in the distance, is in itself most beautiful, and the range of prospects which it commands is of the highest quality and infinitely varied. Such combinations of hill and dale, of wood and water, of buildings and shipping; such a contrast of bustle and repose; in short so excellent a composition of art and nature, if the expression be allowable, had not presented itself in the course of this or any other voyage. From this point also, looking down on the Breakwater, that stupendous work is seen to great advantage, its vastness being decided by the scale of vessels of every size. A scene such as this defies the imagery of mere language, the beholder may gaze until he is mute with admiration; but it is indescribable.

58 VIEW FROM MOUNT EDGCUMBE

Daniell spent a whole day 'perambulating' around the grounds of Mount Edgcumbe. He was now nearing the end of his circumnavigation of the British Isles, and it is interesting to note that, after all that he had seen, he considered this to be the finest 'composition of art and nature'. Indeed it is an extremely peaceful place, although it suffered badly in the severe storms of 1990.

The mile-long breakwater, with a lighthouse at its western end, took 28 years to build and was completed in 1840. In the middle distance is the Great Mew Stone.

59 HAMOAZE FROM MOUNT EDGECUMBE

The Bay properly so called is about four miles in length, from its entrance to its inland extremity at the mouth of the Tamar; its general breadth is about half a mile; the bottom is of mud. The entrance from Plymouth Sound is so intricate and dangerous, that the aid of a pilot is always necessary. The objects represented on the surface of the Bay are ships laid up in ordinary, of which the nearest is the flag-ship.

59 HAMOAZE FROM MOUNT EDGCUMBE

It is surprising how often I have found a public seat in the right place, and so it was here. The afternoon was fine and warm and, apart from the distant hum of the city, the only sound was of sheep grazing. It was enough to send me to sleep . . . and it did. Again, much damage was done in the winter storms, but the trees shown on the left of my picture are possibly the same as those shown in Daniell's view. The obelisk on the near headland features in both pictures and was erected about 1775. It bears no inscriptions and contemporary rumour suggested that it was built by the then Countess of Mount Edgcumbe to commemorate the death of her pet pig. In fact it appears that it was built as a navigational aid. In the distance, on the left, are the railway and road bridges across the River Tamar, the first having been completed in 1859 and the second in 1961.

The definition of 'ships laid up in ordinary' is explained in no. 26.

60 PORT WRINKLE

This is a small village consisting of fishermen's huts, and a curing house for pilchards. Its circular little pier affords the only shelter on this station for boats employed in the fishery, of which not more than three or four belong to this place. Compared with the scenes recently visited, Port Wrinkle presented an aspect by no means attractive.

60 PORT WRINKLE

The harbour wall has been greatly reduced in height but a store-house, which was used for curing pilchards, is still in existence at the end of the road, although in a state of decay. This was a pleasant place in which to spend a quiet afternoon sketching, although the occasional shower was a nuisance. The coastline stretches as far as Looe, with Looe Island on the left; this was bombed in the Second World War by an enemy aircraft whose pilot mistook the island for a British warship.

61 EAST LOOE

In this view, it may be requisite to state, that the object on the extreme verge of the horizon is the Edystone Light-house, distant about 15 miles. Near the centre is the narrow irregular bridge of fifteen arches, which connects East Looe with West Looe. A considerable number of sloops may be occasionally seen at this little port, employed in bringing limestone, or taking away corn. The pilchard fishery is also carried on to some extent.

61 EAST LOOE

It took me a long time to find this view, which is from Trenant Point. At first I thought that it could be reached from West Looe, but this was not possible. Eventually, having travelled much farther inland and walked across numerous fields, I arrived at about the right place. For once I had to employ considerable artistic licence as the gasometer in the foreground was far too prominent. The fifteen-arch, mediaeval bridge was replaced in 1853 by another one 12 feet wide, which, in turn, was widened in 1960.

As in Daniell's view, the Eddystone lighthouse can be seen on the horizon. This is the fifth lighthouse on the Eddystone rocks and was built in 1882.

62 POLPERRO

Polperro is a very busy little town, most oddly situated. There is a narrow entrance, between rocky banks, to the harbour, which affords a safe little shelter for boats when they can get in. On the lower hill, in the centre of the view, is a ruin, said to have been formerly a small chapel. The town is very irregularly built; the inhabitants are mostly fishermen, and in the pilchard season, whatever inclination they may have for cleanliness, they cannot be otherwise than dirty. Of course little can be said of the beauty, and nothing of the elegance of Polperro; but the environs abound in picturesque features, though of a humble kind, such as uncouth cottages, so strangely planted among the rocks, that they seem to have been dropt there, and left to take their chance of a settlement.

62 POLPERRO

There were two ways to approach this subject: one down through the village, the other along the coastal path from Porthallow. At 5.30 a.m. it was a glorious morning so I decided to take the coast walk; it was a long one but well worth the effort. Daniell has foreshortened the western side of the entrance to the harbour, and again he has exaggerated the height of the scenery. The village has become a major tourist attraction, notwithstanding Daniell's comment that little could be said of its beauty.

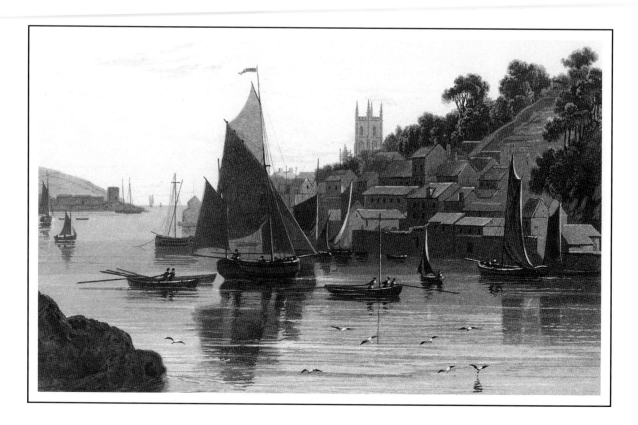

63 FOWEY FROM BODENICK

The building on the left is the castle which once served to protect the harbour. The town stands on the opposite bank of the river Fawy, from whose name it derives its own. The harbour, which its expanded waters form near the town of Fowey, is secure and spacious. For its protection, two square towers were erected by Henry the Fourth on the rocks opposite the harbour and these ruins are still to be seen. The walls are six feet in thickness and they apparently had four floors, each five yards square; they were mounted with cannon. Between them, it is said, that a strong chain was formerly extended, as an additional security to the entrance of the harbour.

63 FOWEY FROM BODINNICK

An early start was necessary if this view was to be seen at the right time of day. There was no immediate access to the point that I wanted to reach as a private property stood in the way and I was not allowed to pass through it – the first time, so far, that permission had been refused. The only route was along the top of the adjoining hillside, past the memorial to Sir Arthur Quiller-Couch, down through dense undergrowth with precarious footholds, and then to a perilous small cliff at the edge of the water. The climb back was even more difficult and I emerged dishevelled and exhausted to the horrified amazement of a lady who was taking her dog for an early morning walk. On the left of my picture there is a small square tower; this is one of the 14th century block-houses, mentioned by Daniell, that were erected on each side of the harbour.

64 FOWEY CASTLE

The present defences of Fowey's harbour are two small bastions of modern erection, and St. Catherine's Fort, built by Henry the Fourth. The castle is situated on a crag, at the western side of the harbour's mouth. At this time, a frigate, and several large ships, were passing down channel; and these, together with the pilchard-boats of Fowey, gave much animation to the scene. To such extent is the fishery carried on here, that in productive seasons nearly thirty thousand hogshead are said to be brought into this port alone. The broken fish, and the refuse of the salt are sold at a certain price by the cart load, and used as manure. The houses of the town are mostly of stone, and extend along the bank of the river for more than a mile; but the streets are so irregular, crooked and narrow, that a carriage can scarcely pass through any of them.

64 FOWEY CASTLE

A pleasant walk through a delightful town brought me to Readymoney Cove, where I found Daniell's view. The ruins of St Catherine's Castle, built during the reign of Henry VIII, stand at the entrance to the harbour. On the right are the remains of the tower depicted by Daniell, which is the companion of the one described in no. 63.

The harbour is busy with many small craft and ocean-going cargo ships that are loaded with china clay at the wharf above the Bodinnick ferry. Fowey was developed by Edward I as a south-western addition to the Cinque Ports and those in East Anglia. However, it became a hotbed of piracy, and Edward IV commanded men from Dartmouth to destroy the ships and harbour.

65 POLKERRIS

The village of Polkerris, with its pier, presented an inviting subject for the pencil. The inhabitants are employed in the pilchard industry. The precipitous bank seen in the view is much worn by the sea, and the pier is much exposed to the violence of the westerly winds. In tempestuous weather the waves beat over it so complete as to form an arch, and on these occasions it often happens that a portion of the structure is washed away.

65 POLKERRIS

It was impossible to reach Daniell's viewpoint because the undergrowth was too dense, so I clambered round the edge of the cliff and completed a pleasant two hours' work. This was almost too long: the tide had risen considerably by the time I had finished, and it was with some difficulty that I was able to return.

Daniell comments on the 'tempestuous weather' that batters these shores, and rough seas are shown in many of his views. During my travels so far there has only been one day when the sea has surged and boiled ferociously. The remains of one of the buildings associated with the pilchard industry, and shown in Daniell's view, can be seen on the edge of the shore.

66 MEVAGISSEY

Mevagissey is certainly very picturesque, but it cannot be called so 'sweet' a spot as some which have been visited during the course of this tour. As its chief dependence is on the pilchard industry it is liable to the privations consequent on an unproductive season. Some years ago a great scarcity prevailed; and the miseries of hunger were augmented by a putrid fever, which proved fatal to many persons. In their distress the fishermen exerted themselves to procure limpets, on which they entirely subsisted, though this kind of food had been previously held in contempt. When the pilchards revisited the bay great quantities were taken; and the opening of the vaults or cellars where the salt was deposited instantly checked the fever; so that after a few days the inhabitants were delivered from both evils.

66 MEVAGISSEY

A most pleasant place to sit on a gloriously hot day, and exactly where Daniell had been. As was to be expected, the town was crowded with visitors and I was glad to have my isolated 'perch' from which to view the scene. This was one of those occasions when it was an advantage to have to choose a single subject as there were many others that caught the eye. The two main piers are basically unchanged though there is now a pleasantly designed building on the nearer one, and an attractive group of buildings at the end of the other.

Leisure craft and fishing boats mingle in the harbour, which for many years was the scene of popular and profitable smuggling.

67 GORRAN HAVEN

Here there is a little pier for the shelter of the pilchard boats. The rocks here and in the neighbourhood are of a bold and picturesque aspect. On the high ground there is a signal-post for the preventive service.

67 GORRAN HAVEN

Modern houses now straggle up the hill from the small village on the right, and I was kindly invited into the one that overlooks the view. This has remained almost unchanged since Daniell's visit on the same day 167 years earlier.

68 PORT LOOE

Port Looe presented one of the wildest scenes on the coast, especially in the existing state of the weather, when heavy sea was tumbling in from the eastward. Between the rocks there is a passage, up which the pilchard boats are drawn high and dry, to be out of reach of the waves. There are seven large boats belonging to this port, which is a place of very little note. About two miles distant, near Penmare Point, is the Gull, or Gray Rock, which, in form and height, is very much like the Mewstone, near Plymouth. Port Looe is particularly well adapted as a haven for the pilchard fishery, on which its inhabitants principally, if not solely, depend. Its position, however, may have offered temptations for contraband traffic, as it has been found necessary to establish here a station for the preventive service.

68 PORTLOE

Daniell visited Portloe on September 8th 1823, and I recorded the same view on the same date 167 years later. The principal building on the right, also depicted in Daniell's view, is the Lugger Hotel, where my wife and I arrived for our honeymoon on September 8th 1957; this present visit coincided with our 33rd wedding anniversary.

Daniell's view is a good example of how he adjusted a scene for pictorial purposes. The pinnacle, which is called the Jacka, is shown above the houses, whereas it is much farther to the left, and less pronounced. Similarly he gives the impression that the hill behind it is much higher. Finally, he compresses the width of the subject so that he can incorporate Gull Rock in the distance.

69 FALMOUTH

Falmouth is situated at the foot of an eminence terminating in a promontory at the extremity of which stands Pendennis Castle. The building in the foreground is the Greenbank Hotel, to which belongs the neighbouring pier. This, being the principal westerly port of the kingdom, is the regular packet station for Spain, Portugal, British America and the West Indies. The entrance to the harbour is completely commanded by Pendennis Castle, which, from its abrupt elevation, nearly three hundred feet above the level of the sea, appears at a distance to be insulated. The fortifications on the north side consist of four defences called cavaliers, mounted with 70 pieces of cannon, on the east is a half-moon battery. On the south, the hill slopes towards the sea, forming a kind of glacis.

69 FALMOUTH

The Greenbank Hotel still exists, but Daniell has reduced its bulk; it is not possible to see the harbour and the hotel at the same time from the selected viewpoint. My view is taken from a small garden in front of the hotel, and the church tower, which was a prominent feature in Daniell's view, can just be seen on the extreme right, above a new development called Admiralty Quay.

Falmouth is one of the world's finest natural harbours and bustles with cargo ships, tugs, yachts, and small passenger ferries, one of which is shown heading for Flushing.

Daniell refers to cavaliers, which are raised defences commanding a view over the country, and a glacis, which is a gentle slope in the fortifications.

70 THE LIZARD

The Lizard light-houses are very conspicuous; though the cliffs on which they stand are of moderate elevation. It should be added, in justice to the persons who superintend them, that they are kept in excellent order, and in an admirable state of cleanliness. This is the southernmost headland of Great Britain, and the perils with which it menaces the mariner render the utility of the beacons established here abundantly manifest. At the base of the cliffs there is a very ugly reef of rocks a few of which are visible at high water.

70 THE LIZARD

There have been more shipwrecks on the rocks off the Lizard than anywhere else round the coast of Britain. The first lighthouse was built in 1619; this was replaced in 1752 and modified in 1903 and, like all the others under the management of Trinity House, is in excellent order.

Just one of the prominent rocks in the foreground of Daniell's view appears to remain. With rocks like these all round this part of Cornwall, it is not surprising that so many ships have met their doom here. It was also here in 1588 that the Spanish Armada was first sighted.

71 MULLYAN COVE

A favourable subject for delineation presented itself at Mullyan Cove. The scenery around is rocky, and as wild as possible. In heavy gales from the South West, the cove affords safe shelter for small vessels, while the Gull Rock protects them from the sudden and dangerous influence of the ground swell. On the day preceding this visit, there had been seventy or eighty at anchor here, perfectly screened from the strong easterly wind that continued to blow. Of the many which tried to round the Lizard some few succeeded, but the others were glad to get back to this safe anchorage.

71 MULLION COVE

This view should have been taken farther down the slope, but another artist was sitting in the exact spot; she is seen on the right. So far she is the only artist I have met during my travels who has been working 'en plein air'. The two great rocks provide marvellous sentinels to the small harbour, but they were not enough to prevent the quays from being damaged in the storms of 1989.

Not long after Daniell's visit, most of the cove's fishing boats were wrecked in a violent gale, but it was not until 1895 that the harbour was built. It is now owned by the National Trust.

72 ST MICHAEL'S MOUNT

At no period had there been so much occasion to rejoice in the continuance of that clear settled weather, which had prevailed ever since the departure from Torquay; for an assemblage of objects presented itself which required the cheering influence of a cloudless sunshine to be seen in perfection. St. Michael's Mount; the little pier with shipping near it; the Bay, studded over with boats, of which at least one hundred might be counted, produced an effect which cannot be described in detail, and must simply be characterized as very beautiful. This view includes the causeway which connects the Mount with the mainland, and which is passable at low water.

72 ST MICHAEL'S MOUNT

This was a comparatively easy subject to draw, and was something of a relief after so many difficult ones. I decided not to wait for the tide to recede, which would have meant a delay of about four hours, but the causeway, linking the Mount to Marazion and shown in Daniell's view, is still there. The outward appearance of the 14th century castle on the peak has hardly changed, although there is a small extension at the eastern end. The fine weather experienced by Daniell since he left Torquay had also accompanied me on my travels along this stretch of coast, and it made me realise how pleasant this country can be when the sun shines – even during the holiday season.

73 PENZANCE

Penzance has a convenient harbour, in which there is a large pier for the security and accommodation of the numerous trading vessels by which it is frequented, as well as the frigates and excise cutters that are stationed here for the purpose of checking, though they cannot totally suppress, the contraband trade which is carried on along this part of the coast, to an unknown extent, and with a combination of boldness and sagacity which would be admirable if directed to a worthy and lawful object. The peculiar salubrity and mild temperature of its air have rendered Penzance a most eligible residence for persons afflicted with pulmonary complaints, and many, who are concerned rather for the preservation than the recovery of their health, have been induced to settle here by the cheapness and excellent quality of the provisions.

73 PENZANCE

One must cross the main London to Penzance railway line near the heliport in order to see this view. By early evening the silhouette of Penzance against the setting sun provided a tranquil end to the day – only to be shattered by a speeding inter-city express and a helicopter returning from the Scilly Isles. It was another moment to reflect on the changes that have taken place since Daniell's travels, and ponder what might happen over the next 167 years.

The large building on the right of Daniell's view was the Chapel of Ease: this was demolished in 1832 and St Mary's Church, which is in the centre of my picture, was built on the same site between 1832 and 1836. On the right is the dome of the Market House which dates from between 1836 and 1838.

74 LAND'S END

On Sunday Sept 14, a concluding visit was paid to the Land's End. The atmosphere was cloudy, and suited this wild scene much better than if it had been clear, with bright sunshine. There was a terrible sea roaring about the Longships light-house. From information obtained on the spot, and which may be readily believed, it appears that in hard gales the lighthouse is frequently hid in the spray, though the rock on which it stands is sixty feet above the level of the sea.

* * * * *

On returning to the point at which the voyage was commenced in the summer of 1813, it was natural to remember the varying hopes of success which attended its progress along the coasts of England, Wales, Scotland and the Western Isles. It may be permitted to observe that those hopes varied, not merely as the toil and hardship became more or less severe, but according to the augmentation or decrease of that public encouragement which was essential to the furtherance and completion of the work. Some persons who evinced an intention to promote its entire success relinquished it as soon as those portions were completed in which local attachments or prepossessions they felt especially interested. This observation is by no means intended to circumscribe or qualify the thanks that are here offered to all who have in any degree favoured the undertaking; but in accepting them, its occasional patrons will readily allow that the largest share of gratitude is due to those friends through whose constant support it has been conducted to its termination.

74 LAND'S END

Fortunately, of the million or so people who visit Land's End each year, very few wander further than the palace of amusements and refreshments that has been developed over the years. It was possible, therefore, to find a secluded spot from which to draw this subject which, basically, has not changed a great deal. The white building on the edge of the cliff is the last house between England and the New World.

Although I still have a long way to go before I complete my circumnavigation of the British Isles, it seemed appropriate to be here on September 14th, which was the precise date of Daniell's arrival here ten years after he set out.

His diary records no strong emotion at having accomplished such an amazing feat, but it must have been an extraordinary moment for him. His closing words are of gratitude to his friends for their constant support to the end of his Voyage. I am barely a quarter of the way through my Voyage, but the interest and encouragement I have received has been most welcome and gratifying.

The tranquillity and generally fine weather during these first two years of travelling along the south coast, together with the constant support and loving companionship of my wife, had made my Voyage a most pleasurable experience. But as I turned the corner at Land's End to continue my travels along the north coast of Cornwall, the gaunt cliffs and stormy seas appeared to be full of foreboding . . . .

INDEX